C000152016

AROUND
SALISBURY
IN OLD PHOTOGRAPHS

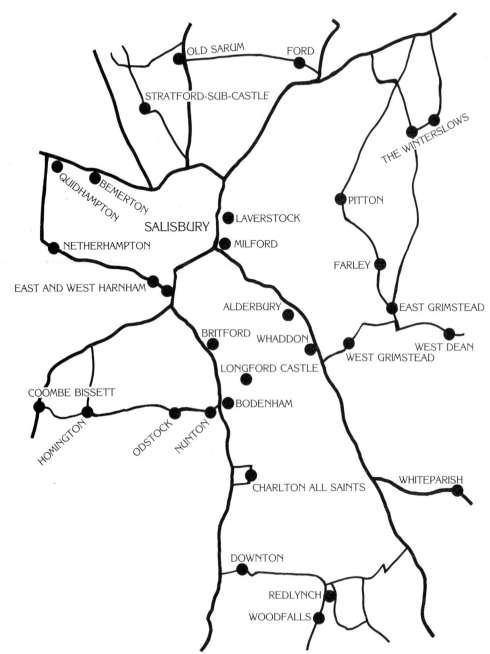

OLD SARUM   FORD

STRATFORD-SUB-CASTLE

THE WINTERSLOWS

QUIDHAMPTON BEMERTON

PITTON

SALISBURY   LAVERSTOCK

NETHERHAMPTON   MILFORD

FARLEY

EAST AND WEST HARNHAM

ALDERBURY   EAST GRIMSTEAD

BRITFORD WHADDON   WEST DEAN

WEST GRIMSTEAD

LONGFORD CASTLE

COOMBE BISSETT   BODENHAM

HOMINGTON   ODSTOCK NUNTON

WHITEPARISH

CHARLTON ALL SAINTS

DOWNTON

REDLYNCH

WOODFALLS

OUR MAP, drawn by Lisa Daniels, shows the area around Salisbury illustrated in this, the third in a series of books depicting Salisbury and south-east Wiltshire in old photographs. Further volumes are planned to include the towns and villages to the north and west of Salisbury. (Map not to scale.)

AROUND
SALISBURY
IN OLD PHOTOGRAPHS

COLLECTED BY
PETER DANIELS

ALAN SUTTON
1989

Alan Sutton Publishing
Gloucester

First published 1989

Copyright © 1989 Peter Daniels

All rights reserved. No part of this publication may be reproduced, stored in a
retrieval system, or transmitted, in any form or by any means, electronic,
mechanical, photocopying, recording or otherwise, without the prior
permission of the publishers and copyright holder

British Library Cataloguing in Publication Data

Around Salisbury in old photographs.
1. Wiltshire. Salisbury, history
I. Daniels, Peter
942.3',9

ISBN 0-86299-665-1

Typesetting and origination by
Alan Sutton Publishing
Printed in Great Britain by
Dotesios Printers Limited

CONTENTS

PETER DANIELS, 'THE OLD PICTURE DETECTIVE', with a 1908 Moto-Sacoche engine-assisted pedal cycle from the Charlie Knight Collection. The photograph was taken after the Salisbury Hospital Carnival on 4 June 1989.

INTRODUCTION

Today in this photographic anniversary year, 1989, black and white and colour photography is within the reach of everyone. From simple cameras to sophisticated semi-professional equipment costing many hundreds of pounds, we have to thank William Henry Fox Talbot of Lacock House, Wiltshire. It is 150 years since he perfected the negative/positive photographic process, having read on 31 January 1839 his paper 'Some Account of the Art of Photogenic Drawing' to the Royal Society. For the very first time this exclusive society was made aware of his 'Calotype' process. In the following four years Fox Talbot continued his experiments until he was able to produce paper images of a consistent standard.

In Peter Daniels' first collection of photographs, we were given an insight into the everyday life of the citizens of Salisbury during the latter part of the nineteenth century through to the first half of the twentieth. In this new collection of carefully selected photographs we are shown village life over a similar period. Mr Daniels, who is known in Salisbury as 'The Old Picture Detective', has gathered together over 250 pictures illustrating the social history of the villages and hamlets of south-east Wiltshire which will provoke some nostalgia. Many of the photographs have come from private collections and are being shown to the public for the first time. The changes shown by these photographs, stretching over a hundred years, from 1847 to the 1950s, are similar from village to village. Because of the individuality of each of these communities they all differ and will be equally fascinating not only to those people who were born and lived, and still continue to live in the villages, but to all lovers of the English countryside.

Many changes have taken place in village life during the period covered by the illustrations in this latest volume. The village churches which were once the centre of the community now play a much smaller role, many have been closed, converted into homes. Many of the rectories and vicarages have been sold, for there is no longer a parson for each church. Grouped together they are served by a team-ministry, in many instances the church is open only for one service on a Sunday and in some cases there is not even a weekly service. Village schools have also been the subject of increasing economic pressures. A number have been closed and in the next few years, almost certainly, a great many more will suffer the same fate. Many children no longer walk to school but are 'bussed' considerable distances to newer and larger establishments.

Many of the railway stations disappeared under Dr Beeching's axe and bus companies are finding it increasingly difficult to run a viable service. Not everyone in these remote communities is able, either for financial or other reasons, to own a motor car, one wonders if there is not an opportunity for enterprising individuals to re-introduce the services of a carrier such as James Colborne who can be seen on page 11 in this book. The daily life of the villagers has become much less arduous, with the supply of piped water saving those exhausting journeys to and from the village pumps and springs regardless of the weather. The Alderbury water supply, as an example, was a gift from the Earl of Radnor to the people of the village; a photograph of the 1902 inauguration ceremony is shown in Section Five. Light is now available at the touch of a switch, we are no longer dependent on smokey oil lamps or guttering candles. Village post offices had begun to disappear but in some communities they are being re-opened in village shops and pubs, providing a service of inestimable value, especially to the elderly.

Finally, yet another change in village life has been the arrival of new families from outside Wiltshire. The breadwinners are prepared to commute daily to offices as far away as London in order to be able to live in the tranquillity of the countryside. The impact they have made is very obvious, with the modernization of old churches, rectories, schools and chapels, the conversion of barns and the erection of 'executive style' houses. Their Range Rovers and BMWs are to be seen amongst the more humble motor cars of the village.

Mr Daniels is again to be congratulated for all the wonderful illustrations he has discovered. Many he has acquired for his own ever-growing and comprehensive collection. Others he has found in private collections and we must thank those kind individuals who have allowed their photographs to be used and by so doing are giving much pleasure to all who read this book. There are still many thousands of old photographs, books, directories, newspapers and documents hidden away in family albums, drawers, cupboards and attics. It is sad to think that many of these items will be destroyed or thrown away when their owners die: once gone they cannot be replaced. Perhaps this is the time for all of you to look these items out and get in touch with Mr Daniels so that he may have them copied, preserving them for the enjoyment of our children and our children's children.

GEOFFREY CROWE
Salisbury 1989

SECTION ONE

East and West Harnham, Netherhampton and Quidhampton

OUR JOURNEY BEGINS AT THE HARNHAM GATE, one of the three entrances to the Close. This photograph of around 1909 shows pupils of the Choristers' School ready for an outing.

A 1909 PICTURE OF CHORISTERS PUNTING on the Avon, copied from a magic lantern slide. A man can be seen carrying a ladder across Ayleswade (Harnham) Bridge.

THE BRIDGE AT HARNHAM, 25 April 1908. Up to 14 inches of snow lay in the district, the heaviest fall Salisbury had experienced since the great storm of 1881.

HOMEWARD BOUND. James Colborne, the Cranborne carrier, crossing the Avon on a market day at Salisbury in around 1925. His horse had been stabled for the day at the William IV Inn, Milford Street.

HENRY MORRIS WAS LANDLORD OF THE SWAN INN, when this picture was taken in around 1891. The donkey carts, returning to Coombe Bissett and Odstock, can be seen passing the inn near Ayleswade Bridge.

TAXIS AT THE SWAN HOTEL after the First World War. The wire-wheeled open car is a Wolseley Torpedo Tourer, the other a Ford Model T landaulette. Frederick Hallett, proprietor of the hotel, operated this taxi service.

KING GEORGE V'S SILVER JUBILEE CELEBRATIONS, May 1935. The 'League of Beauty' float near Bown's dairy in Harnham Road. The picture was taken by Charles Bridle an accomplished amateur photographer. His daughter Mary is sitting nearest the camera and her sister Joyce is standing at the back.

THE ROSE AND CROWN INN, 1909, Mrs M. Smith, the landlady, is nearest the camera with her sister Mrs Preston. Charlie Musslewhite and Joe Gale are standing under the sign to the left of the slot machines. You could buy a bar of chocolate or have yourself weighed for just 1d.

EAST HARNHAM VILLAGE, 1907. The cottages to the right have changed very little, but on the other side of the road it is a different story. The trees and fences have gone and a row of modern houses now stand here.

WILLIAM MORGAN AND FAMILY AT HARNWOOD, 1916. Harnwood House was the home of Godfrey Locker-Lampson MP where Bill Morgan was gardener. Bill is pictured here with his wife, Lilly, and their children, Ethel, Lillie, Oliver and Gwen.

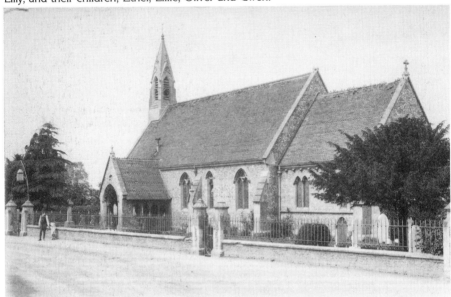

ALL SAINTS' CHURCH at East Harnham, 1902. The Revd Geoffrey Hill was vicar of this church and St George's at West Harnham from 1891 to 1925.

A SCOUT MOTOR CAR at West Harnham, 1909. Caroline and Clifford Radcliffe are pictured with their dark blue 20 hp Roi de Belge tourer, AM 1343, outside their home at No. 81 Harnham Road. The car was made at the Scout Motor Works, Bemerton.

CLIFFORD HERBERT RADCLIFFE, Chairman and Director of The Scout Motor Company. Born at Balderstone Hall, Rochdale in 1878, he moved to Salisbury in 1908. For many years he was churchwarden at East Harnham, Secretary of Salisbury Lawn Tennis and Croquet Club and a popular member of South Wilts. Golf Club. He was killed in a tragic accident at the motor works on 16 September 1915.

WEST HARNHAM VILLAGE during the First World War. The three cottages on the right-hand side were called Elim, Middle Thatch and Bohemian; the latter is now renamed The Old Cottage. The large house in the background is where the manager of Powling's poultry food factory lived.

ELIM COTTAGE in around 1917. It was quite usual at this time for people to have a picture of their house taken by a professional photographer. Copies could then be sent to friends. The sundial and other pieces of garden furniture pictured here have survived.

AEC 'MAMMOTH MAJOR 8' at John Lampard's West Harnham depot, 1935. Mr Lampard's first AEC was WV 8855, the first of many, they were strong reliable wagons. His fleet was always immaculate and the envy of many haulage contractors. A cash and carry now operates on this site.

JOHN LAMPARD WITH HIS FIRST LEYLAND in 1934. The QE2, as she was known, arrived at the yard as a chassis, the van body was assembled and fitted at the depot workshop. Mr Lampard started his business when he returned from the First World War by purchasing an ex-war department lorry. He soon acquired a second and then, after buying new vehicles, he eventually had a fleet of 22. In 1948, along with many other private haulage contractors, his business was nationalized and became part of British Road Services.

DISASTROUS FLOODS AT WEST HARNHAM, Monday, 12 November 1894. Our picture shows that the area around the Three Crowns was badly affected. The pleasure boats that had been stored for the winter were hurriedly put to work.

SALISBURY CATHEDRAL FROM WEST HARNHAM, 1906. A large willow tree now provides a little shade for the ducks when they rest from swimming in the waters near the Old Mill.

THE OLD HARNHAM BESOM BOYS CLUB, portrayed by schoolchildren from East and West Harnham, June 1927. The children are ready to take part in the Salisbury 700th anniversary procession. Their leader is Bill Musslewhite and among the boys are Sidney Edgington, Charles Jago and Fred Larcombe.

HARNHAM RESERVES FOOTBALL TEAM for the 1923–4 season, the boys' names have not been recorded. The compiler would be pleased to hear from anyone with information on this or any of the pictures in this book.

MIDDLE STREET AT WEST HARNHAM, 1906. It lies only a mile or so from Salisbury centre yet here it is in the countryside. Out of view to the right are the fields where Rueben Davis kept his cart horses. Daisy, one of Rueben's daughters now lives in a bungalow built on these fields.

RUEBEN AND ELIZABETH DAVIS with four of their twelve children, photographed on their smallholding at Netherhampton sometime before the First World War. Reg is standing to the left with his dog and Daisy, George and Tom are in the cart.

RUEBEN DAVIS' HEAVY HORSES and their keepers in 1921. The animals were kept in a field next to Meadow Cottages in Middle Street, West Harnham (see picture on opposite page). Rueben stands to the right next to his sons, Reg and George, Jack Major and Jack Parsons stand to the left.

PLAYTIME AT NETHERHAMPTON HOUSE BOARDING SCHOOL, c. 1875. The boys, aged nine to fifteen, were taught by Joel Douty of Wilton who founded the school in around 1870. He continued to teach until his death in 1884 when he was succeeded by Edward Douty.

NETHERHAMPTON VILLAGE in the 1920s. In the middle distance, between the man and St Catherine's church, is the Elementary School which was built in 1856. Miss Alice Clark was the schoolmistress.

ROWDENS AT NETHERHAMPTON. The home of Mrs Dora H. Robertson, author of *Sarum Close*. In December 1937 she sent this photograph to a friend telling her that at long last the book was to be published.

QUEEN ELIZABETH may not have slept here, but Miss Sivyour did. A 1910 postcard with this message: 'Dear Uncle, Hoping all is well, I am well, I like it at Netherhampton very much. This is where I live. Your loving niece, A. Sivyour.'

ST GEORGE'S DAY AT NETHERHAMPTON, Wednesday, 12 June 1912. The celebrations began with dinner, for men only, in the schoolroom followed by a carnival in front of Netherhampton House. Pictured are J. Oliver and C. Frampton with their moonraker's cart.

DOROTHY AND GRAHAM GARLAND, attended as carnival king and queen. At Netherhampton House in the afternoon the children of the village were entertained to tea by Henry Newbolt (there is a breathless hush). The event was organized to raise money for Salisbury Infirmary.

QUIDHAMPTON VILLAGE in around 1913. Alfred Young's blacksmith's shop can be seen in the middle of the picture, his advertising board states: 'Horses shod using all the latest improvements'. The smithy is now Elm Cottage.

ALBION COTTAGES AT QUIDHAMPTON, before the First World War. To the left is one of the five village pumps. The cottages have now been replaced by bungalows.

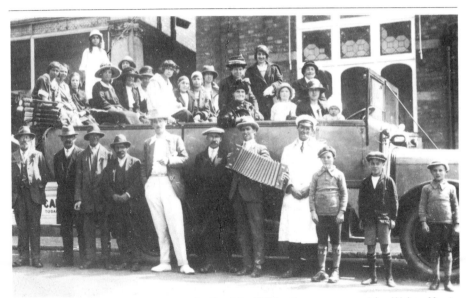

CHARABANC OUTING TO BOURNEMOUTH in the late 1920s. It was arranged by Walter Harris, landlord of the White Horse, who hired the Daimler from Sparrow and Vincent. The trippers were entertained by accordianist Walter (Walt) Cook.

A TRIP TO THE SEASIDE just before the Second World War. This time the Quidhampton party enjoyed a more comfortable ride in a modern saloon coach. The girls in the centre of the picture are three of Mr and Mrs Stokes' twelve children.

EDWARDIAN ELEGANCE AT QUIDHAMPTON in 1910. Clara Jane Price is pictured with her daughters, Clara Florence Emily and Martha Isobella Charlotte. (A portrait of their father is reproduced below.) The family lived at The Poplars.

CHARLES PALK LORAINE PRICE, photographer. Charles fell in love with Clara Jane when she called to have her picture taken at his studio in Hythe, Kent. The couple married and moved to Sherborne, Dorset and eventually to Quidhampton. It was at this time that Charles opened a studio in North Street, Wilton. He later emigrated to Canada.

RACEHORSE STABLING AT QUIDHAMPTON in the last century. There was much activity in the area during the days before and after Salisbury race meetings. Many racehorse owners lodged their animals at the numerous stables in the village. This photograph, by Charles Price, is believed to have been taken behind one of Charles Holly's establishments, the Bell or the White Horse.

Bemerton, Stratford-sub-Castle, Old Sarum and Ford

YOUNG AND CAREFREE. Taken in 1913, this picture shows children paddling and fishing for tiddlers in the stream below Long Bridge. Harnham Hill can be seen in the distance.

LONG BRIDGE AND SALISBURY CATHEDRAL, autumn 1930. A middle-aged couple stop for a while to enjoy the tranquility of this beautiful scene.

BOATING NEAR FISHERTON MILL in 1914. We were unable to discover the identity of this young lady. Was she the daughter of Edward Bowle the miller?

CHILDREN ON THE BANKS OF THE NADDER at Bemerton in 1912. Perhaps these children from Bemerton Elementary School were taking part in a natural history lesson. Schoolmaster Fred Harris is keeping an eye on them. South Wilts. Dairy and the pumping station can be seen to the right.

CHURCH LANE, BEMERTON, in 1929. Group Captain Henry Busteed lived to the right in Swiss Cottage, now Cherbury. His neighbour, John Manfield, resided at Myrtle Cottage.

A VICTORIAN VIEW OF BEMERTON. The people of Wiltshire call this George Herbert's Church. It is hardly ever referred to by its dedication of St Andrew's. On the right is the rectory where Herbert lived.

MOURNERS AT ST JOHN'S CHURCH, Bemerton? The floral tributes are thought to be for Joseph Norton who died on 10 November 1908 aged 75 years. There is only one boy in the group and no black clothing is being worn.

FIRE FIGHTING COMPETITIONS at Bemerton, Thursday, 29 July 1934. The Salisbury Volunteer Fire Brigade were celebrating their Golden Jubilee. A midday luncheon was followed by a procession of old and new fire engines. Competitions were held at the South Wilts. Cricket Ground in the afternoon. This picture shows the motor pump drill.

THE ESCAPE LADDER DRILL. Councillor Rambridge presented a cup to the winning team. The third drill, for the engineers, was won by fireman Albert Noyce with a best time of 16 seconds.

MILK BY MOTOR, 1926. Freddy Foot proudly stands by his Morris 8 cwt van at Tower House Farm, Bemerton. The standard factory van, complete with electric lighting and pneumatic tyres, cost just £167 10s.

THE DAIRY HERD AT TOWER HOUSE FARM, Bemerton, in around 1927. The illustration is a copy of an advertising postcard promoting tuberclin tested milk. By the mid-1930s the firm had opened a retail shop in Castle Street and a milk bar in the Canal.

WILTON ROAD APRIL 1930. One of Walter Chalke's timber waggons can be seen returning to South Newton. He was engaged in felling elm trees that were damaged during the gale of Sunday 12 January.

THE BRIDGE TO STRATFORD-SUB-CASTLE, 1908. Avonside House, the home of Arthur Bruce Russell Davies, can be seen to the left. He was churchwarden at St Lawrence's for 42 years. The photograph was taken by Frederick Futcher whose portrait is featured on page 159.

A STEAM AGRICULTURAL ENGINE at Stratford-Sub-Castle. The photograph was taken at the end of the nineteenth century, at Windmill Path, Parsonage Farm. The steam engine was a comparatively modern tool, but the design of the pitchfork held by the young man on the right had been employed for centuries.

SHEEP SHEARING IN A BARN AT PARSONAGE FARM in around 1907. Albert Kerley is standing second from the left and William Kerley second from the right. Now try and pick them out in the picture opposite.

THRESHING AT PARSONAGE FARM, at the turn of the century. Here is that steam engine again, this time driving the threshing machine. Francis Carey worked the farm from the late 1800s until around 1920 when Reg Coggan took over; Patrick, his grandson, is still farming here.

STRATFORD-SUB-CASTLE MILL in 1897. Barnes Durell was miller here during the last years of the nineteenth century. Both the photographs on this page were taken by Clement Osmond of London Road, Salisbury.

BOATING ON THE AVON NEAR STRATFORD MILL in 1897. The unknown boater-hatted boater was obviously a friend of Clement Osmond for he appears on a number of Clement's early photographs. We are fortunate that he has left us a fascinating pictorial record of life in the last century.

CORONATION CELEBRATIONS at Stratford-Sub-Castle, Wednesday, 28 June 1911. A flagstaff was purchased and erected in the school playground as a permanent reminder of the event. The baby in the pram in the right-hand corner is Ron Kerley.

MISS HARMAN AND CHARLES SHEPHERD in 1861. Charles was the foreman at Parsonage Farm. Soon after these portrait photographs were taken Miss Harman became Mrs Charles Shepherd.

STRATFORD-SUB-CASTLE POST OFFICE, 1913. Mrs Sabina Newman, the postmistress, was up before 6.30 a.m. six days a week to receive the mail from Salisbury. The post office was closed by the mid-1920s and has since become a private house, formerly Morton and now Farthing Cottage.

EXCAVATIONS AT OLD SARUM, 1909–15. Within the first two years the Society of Antiquaries had revealed the plan of the medieval castle. Our photograph, showing the interior plinth of the Great Tower, dates from 1910.

THE GUARD ROOM at the entrance to the inner castle, 1910. This postcard was sent to Miss D. Rowthorne at the Eye and Ear Infirmary at Portsmouth. A part of the message reads: 'I'll send another of the excavations next time, its been a bit of bother to get any at all, have been waiting ages for this card', signed Reg.

STAIRS TO THE TOWER, 1910. These three illustrations of the excavations at Old Sarum are from a series of postcards produced by F. Futcher and Son.

VICTORY CELEBRATIONS AT OLD SARUM ISOLATION HOSPITAL, June 1946. These happy youngsters were invited to a victory tea-party at the hospital. Just one of the many celebrations which took place around Salisbury (there were also street parties, bonfires, processions and firework displays).

THE FIRST MOTOR AMBULANCE IN THE DISTRICT, 1912. The dark blue 19.6 hp conveyance was built for the isolation hospital by the Scout Motor Company. The vehicle was designed to carry two stretcher patients, the driver, a doctor plus two sitting patients or nurses. Miss Jackson was the driver during the First World War.

MISS O. WAINWRIGHT AND MISS ASHFORD during the Second World War, pictured with the Austin ambulance at the Salisbury and District Isolation Hospital. Nurse Wainwright, who is holding Sally, left the hospital in May 1944. The crew and patient arrangements were similar to the Scout ambulance.

THE OLD WATER MILL AT FORD in 1914. Edward Griffin had been the miller from the late 1800s right up to the First World War when John Griffin took over. Griffin Mill Cottage can be seen to the right.

JESSIE, JANE BOSWELL'S DAUGHTER, at the cottage, Home Farm, Ford, in the 1920s. Jane Boswell began selling groceries and cigarettes from this cottage in around 1927. Later her sons Ernest and Kenneth sold logs but changed activities, during the 1930s, to supplying sand and gravel (from their pits at Whaddon and Godshill). It is now a flourishing business employing 18 workers with a fleet of 12 lorries.

A LOVELY STUDIO PORTRAIT OF JANE BOSWELL, taken in around 1905.

ST THOMAS' BRIDGE AT FORD in 1912. The cottage to the left over the bridge has since disappeared. A horse-drawn water tanker can be seen approaching from the London side. The photograph was taken by Henry Buckle who was in business at Dews Road, Salisbury.

Pitton, Farley and the Winterslows

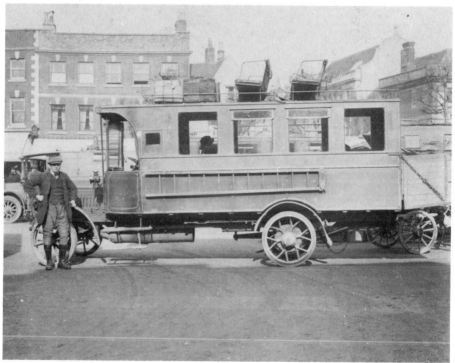

THE WINTERSLOW BUS IN SALISBURY MARKET PLACE, March 1921. Edwin Knight ran a reliable service to Salisbury Market, starting out from the Crooked Billet pub at Winterslow. His 1917, 28 hp Dennis carrier's van, AM 3712, was often to be seen parked in front of the Council Chamber (now the Guildhall). The ladder was used to reach the roof seats. Can you imagine riding up top through those narrow country lanes?

CORNER OF WHITE HILL AND THE GREEN, PITTON, 1914. The house behind the trees to the left is now called Bunbury. Three young men can be seen lounging on the bank outside Netherhill Thatch; this cottage has been tastefully restored and looks very pretty today.

THE GREEN, PITTON, 1916. The cottages to the left are gone and modern houses have replaced them. Glenside, the nearest cottage on the right, is in front of Hillside, an old shoemaker's cottage of the 1800s and probably the home of James Barnett.

THE PITTON BRASS BAND, taken at around the time of the First World War. Concerts were held, mostly on Saturday evenings, at Davids Garden Field where the villagers would assemble near the old elm tree.

ARTHUR AND WALTER WHITE, PITTON WOODMEN. Father and son, employed on the Clarendon estate, are sawing up a mature elm tree that had blown down at Inglewood during a storm in January 1930. Glebe House can be seen in the distance.

MORRIS BAUGH, THE BAKER, delivering to Pitton homes in the 1930s. The hand carts were a common sight in many villages until well after the Second World War. This one was owned by Stanley Horner, the village baker, grocer and corn merchant. The snap was taken by Edith Whitlock.

STANLEY HORNER'S BAKERY VAN at Pitton in around 1934/5. Bob Smith and Dick (the pony) were the best of friends and for a number of years they delivered bread in the Clarendon area. On occasions Bob's wife, Violet, would go along for the ride and she remembers well the happy times they shared together.

THE PITTON ROYAL MAIL VAN in 1913. Many of the village mail carts were housed at Salisbury. The pony and cart featured here was leased from William Henry Baker of St Paul's Road, Salisbury. He stabled the animals, garaged the vehicles and provided lodgings for the postmen.

FARLEY IN FESTIVAL MOOD. It is thought this colourfully dressed group are preparing to celebrate the 1902 coronation of King Edward VII and Queen Alexandra. Victor Parsons, in the Peirrot oufit was, with his father, always to the forefront when it came to organizing celebrations in Farley. Such occasions included processions headed by the Alderbury Band, fancy dress parades, sporting events, a festive tea for the ladies and children rounded off by a supper for the men of the village.

THE ROCKING HORSE AT FARLEY ELEMENTARY SCHOOL in around 1909. Gertie Huxter and Winnie Keevil stand to the left of the picture, the jockey is Dorothy Olding, and at the horse's head, Mary (Cissie) Read. The children were taught by Louise Parsons and Girtie Waters.

THE FARLEY CELEBRATIONS for the coronation of King George VI and Queen Elizabeth, May 1937. Dora Penny (dressed as Britannia) stands near her sister, Mary Elizabeth, who is sitting in the chariot. Mary Elizabeth and her brother George (John Bull) each received a prize for being the youngest Elizabeth and George.

THE MARRIAGE of Victor Emanuel Parsons and Fanny Hayter Gay. Both were from farming families. Victor farmed first at Farley and later at Whiteparish, Fanny's family were from East Grimstead. The picture was taken in the gardens of Church Farm house at Farley.

SARAH JANE PARSONS (née Packer) in 1908. Mrs Parsons had four children all of whom can be seen in the above photograph. Victor is the groom and of the five bridesmaids, three were his sisters Florence, Louise and Elizabeth.

NEWHOLME AT FARLEY at around the turn of the century. Mr Parsons senior is standing at the gate with his youngest daughter, Florence. The house was formerly known as Newmans Farm.

EMANUEL PARSONS in 1908. The portrait photographs of Emanuel and his wife, Sarah, were taken by James Jarvis at the Royal Central Photo. Co. studios at No. 38 The High Street, Salisbury.

A LOVELY WEDDING PHOTOGRAPH commemorating the marriage of Alfred William Parsons and Ada Sarah Warren in 1896. Alfred, a teacher at Fisherton Anger school, moved to Hillside House at Farley at the time of his appointment as Parish Registrar.

HILLSIDE HOUSE a few years later. Patrick Crozier-Cole, the present owner, recently found written on a discarded floorboard the following: 'This house was built in the years 1905–6 by E.H. Pragnell of this parish for Mr Fred Parsons' signed, George Penn.

CHURCH ROAD, FARLEY, during the First World War. Once the children had spotted the photographer they soon stopped playing with their hoops, they had probably never seen a photographer at work before. The house to the left, now known as Our Home, was once the Ilchester Arms Inn.

HAYMAKING AT HILLCROFT FARM, Farley, in 1935. The farm was worked by Thomas Penny who was equally well-known for his regular carrier service to Salisbury on Tuesdays. Most carriers used covered vans but Thomas preferred an open platform cart, pulled by Kit, a very popular carthouse, particularly among the children.

THE HOOK AND GLOVE INN at Farley, after 1914. Mr Hayward, who is standing by the gate, appeared in contemporary directories as George Hayward, Beer Retailer. The pub was rebuilt later and now stands much nearer to the road.

THE FARLEY HOSPITAL AND WARDENRY in 1917. Standing in the centre of the picture is the Revd Charles Matthews Gay who had been appointed vicar and warden just a few days before this photograph was taken. Farley hospital was founded by Sir Stephen Fox in 1682 to accommodate six poor parishioners, three men and three women.

THE HORSESHOE PUB in The Street, West Winterslow, in around 1913 when Philip Liney was landlord. The thatched cottage next to the Horseshoe has been replaced by a modern house known as Stone Banks. The pub is now a private residence called Horseshoe House on which an advertisement for Strong's Ales can still be seen.

AFTER THE OPENING OF THE NEW RECREATION GROUND at Winterslow, June 1905. The children of Winterslow's elementary schools had a great old time. There were around 140 children attending the two schools at this time.

WINTERSLOW FLOWER SHOW AND ODDFELLOWS FÊTE, Friday, 24 July 1908. This, the third event of its kind, was organized as a joint venture between Winterslow Horticultural Society and the Hand-in-Hand Lodge of the Independent Order of Oddfellows. The local schoolchildren were always made welcome and they are pictured here in Rectory field, owned by farmer John King.

WINTERSLOW BAPTIST CHAPEL OUTING TO SOUTHSEA, 1934/5. The children, from the left are: Gerald Stone, Barbara Reeves, Joyce Lampard, Gwen Pennells, Alan Russell, Bob Lampard, Ken Ludlow and in the pushchair, Freda Ludlow. Christina Lampard is at the back, fifth from the right.

ALL SAINTS' CHURCH, West Winterslow, in around 1905. The rector, Revd James Coombe Noel, left Winterslow soon after this photograph was taken, he had been the incumbent since 1893. He was succeeded as rector by Revd Charles Templar Wheat.

THE WINTERSLOW MOTOR CARRIER AT SALISBURY in March 1921, parked outside the Roe Buck Inn in the Canal. The Winterslow and District Motor Service was operated by Parsons Brothers of Middle Winterslow. Their vehicle made regular trips to Salisbury, chiefly for the Tuesday and Saturday Markets. The bus, which was registered as a hackney carriage, was formerly double-decker bus number 816 of the London General Omnibus Company, the chassis is the LGOC B-type.

LIGHT INDUSTRY AT WINTERSLOW in around 1910. The Duchess of Hamilton was president of the Winterslow Spinning and Weaving Industry Society, Louise Witt was secretary. Mr Reynolds the overseer was responsible for three hand looms.

TAR SPRAYING AT LIVERY ROAD Winterslow in the 1930s. The tar was heated in the horse-drawn boiler and then sprayed onto the road. Stone chippings were then shovelled from the cart onto the tarred surface.

WINTERSLOW POST OFFICE ON MIDDLETON ROAD, erected in 1901, now a private residence called Old Post Office Cottage. Alexander Hardy was the sub-postmaster when this picture was taken in 1906, it is thought he may have been the chap on the extreme left.

HORNER'S CENTRAL STORES at Middle Winterslow. Tom Horner was a shopkeeper in the last century and by 1905, the date of this picture, he was well established on this site. To the left of the shopfront is a young man holding up a poster advertising Ward's Seeds and on the extreme left is Louis Roger's blacksmith's shop.

RUFUS CLARKE'S CART IN GUNVILLE ROAD, 1906. Rufus was the village wheelwright, his house, now known as Lime Cottage, can be seen to the right. Many of these houses were built around the turn of the century, including Woodleaze which stands a little way down the hill to the left.

A RECORD SNOW STORM at Winterslow, 25 April 1908. Our picture shows William Reeves, the Parish Clerk, and a friend at King's Corner. The Old Manor House is just visible through the snow laden trees, John King lived here.

THE WINTERSLOW HUT on the main road to London in 1907, now the Pheasant Hotel. The host, Francis Edward Williams, retailed ales, wines and spirits supplied by John Folliott's Brewery of Rollestone Street, Salisbury.

Laverstock, East and West Grimstead, West Dean and Whiteparish

FRAMPTON'S DAIRY CART near Cow Lane, Laverstock, 1909. Leonard is on the float alongside Frank, his younger brother. The rounds took them to Laverstock and Milford, their father Robert Frampton had started the business some years earlier.

THE GREEN AT LAVERSTOCK, 1913. Elizabeth Uphill's post office, now Elmcott, is on the left. Frances Kellow, builder and undertaker ran her business from the house on the far right. This photograph was taken by Charles H. May of Porton whose 3½ hp Premier motor-cycle is parked outside the post office.

LAVERSTOCK VILLAGE, in around 1910. The cottages nearest to the camera on the right have gone but Lynwood Cottages in Duck Lane survive. The Thatch and Church Road are on the left. The man at the front of our picture has a lawn-mower in his wheelbarrow.

THE RIVER BOURNE AT LAVERSTOCK, in around 1911, with the mill house in the distance. Phillip Goddard, miller and fellmonger, occupied the house in the later part of the last century, but when this picture was taken Edward Blake was the miller.

THE HILL AT LAVERSTOCK, 1907. Neil Herbert lived here until 1903 when a Mrs Coates took up residence. From 1925 to 1960 it was the home of Major Bernard Byles. The house was built on land now occupied by Dalewood Rise, Silverwood Drive and Paddock Way.

THE JOYCE BROTHERS AT GLEBE FARM, East Grimstead, after the Second World War. Ted can be seen on the left, Wallace in the centre and Harry on the trailer. The brothers were working with a new Fordson tractor, FWV 617.

GOAT POWER at Grimstead, in around 1933. Elsie Penny was nursemaid to the children of Walter Wadsworth of Walden House, West Grimstead. Our picture shows her with two youngsters as they set off for an outing in the goat cart.

ALFRED T.W. GAY, 1881–1953. Alfred, who farmed at East Grimstead, is pictured outside Manor Farm House in around 1906. The photograph was taken by Harry Marlow Rewse of Water Lane, Salisbury.

HAMPSHIRE DOWN SHEEP on the downs at East Grimstead, just before the First World War. The sheep, bred by Alfred Gay, were always much admired and won him numerous awards over the years, mostly at the sheep fairs held annually at Britford.

WEST GRIMSTEAD BRICKYARD, in around 1907. This most interesting picture was taken by Charlie May of Porton. A photograph of Charlie appears on page 157.

STAFF AND TRANSPORT AT KNIGHTWOOD BRICKYARD in 1920. Driver Harry Turner can be seen to the right, sitting on his mate's shoulders. His conveyance is an ex-war department FWD army lorry. Sid Newel and his son are in the centre, holding brick moulds.

WEST GRIMSTEAD POST OFFICE, 1914. This was Henry Penn's establishment on the corner of Church Street and Dean Road. It housed the post office, a bakery, grocery and a recruiting office for the Royal Navy and Royal Marines.

DELIVERY CARTS AT WEST GRIMSTEAD, 1908. John Steven Penn set up his bakery business at around the turn of the century. His main competition came from Edmund Hopkins who had been trading as a baker and carrier since the 1880s.

REMEMBERING THE BRAVE who fell in the First World War. The dedication of the war memorial at West Grimstead in 1920. In memory of Pte. R. Beauchamp, H. Bundy, W. Coombs, W. Gumbleton and F. Light. More recently, a plaque was placed here to the memory of Second World War bomber pilot Frank R. Harwood.

'WINGS FOR VICTORY WEEK' AT EAST GRIMSTEAD, May 1943. US soldiers visited the village and helped to raise £2,143 6s. The event was opened by Major J. Morrison. Gwen Joyce is the little girl on the right holding a flower arrangement.

A SOLDIER, A THATCHER AND A LAND-GIRL at East Grimstead, May 1943. Sergeant James Mason of Dublin, Georgia, USA, is pictured with Victor Fry, a lifelong resident of East Grimstead. Miss Daisy Stubbington of Plumstead, London, is on the right; she worked on the land at Whitehouse farm.

'THE BLUE BELLE' at West Grimstead, May 1929. Archie and Cedric Curtis acquired the REO bus, MW 4352, in April 1929. The two-tone blue 20-seater ran a daily service to Salisbury. From the left: John 'Peggy' Curtis; Archie; conductor, Victor Early and Cedric. John's wife Ellen is looking over the hedge.

CHAPEL HILL AT WEST GRIMSTEAD, 1906. Walter Browne's little post office, which is pictured just right of centre, later became a parcel office for the local carriers. The thatched cottage on the right is now known as Orchard House.

WEST GRIMSTEAD ELEMENTARY SCHOOL GROUP, 1907. The school was erected in 1850 to accommodate 60 children. At the time of our picture Miss Daisy Parsons was headmistress.

KNIGHTWOOD COTTAGES AT WEST GRIMSTEAD, 1907. The tied houses were built by the Earl of Radnor in around 1860 for Longford estate gamekeepers. William Turner and members of his family can be seen in the garden.

WORKERS AT WEST DEAN, around the time of the First World War. The Salisbury, Semley and Gillingham Dairy was operating from around 1895 until the mid-1920s. Its first manager was William Harwood who was succeeded in turn by John Sherrin (1906) and Edwin Griffiths (1910). Our picture shows John Marsh the foreman and his daughter, Olive, who can be seen between Colin Kerley and Edmund Carter.

THE SALISBURY, SEMLEY AND GILLINGHAM DAIRY in around 1895. The donkey regularly hauled the churn cart across to the railway station and back completely unaccompanied, he just needed to be pointed in the right direction.

A BUSY DAY AT WEST DEAN in the last century. The corner of the SS & G dairy can be seen to the right with the station and lodge appearing in the distance. The owners of the ponies and traps had probably just met a train.

A GENERAL VIEW OF WEST DEAN, 1902. The dairy building on the extreme left is now King George's Hall. In the distance, beyond the signal box, stood the post office where Ellen Coombs was the postmistress. The red brick station house looked immaculate at this time.

LONDON AND SOUTH WESTERN RAILWAY STATION at West Dean, 1908. Charles Kennett was station master. The signal box was taken away some years ago and is now safely preserved by an enthusiast. The 4–4–0 locomotive is seen on the westbound track, heading for Salisbury.

THE CHILWORTH AND STONEHAM HARRIERS MEET AT DEAN STATION, Wednesday, 7 March 1906. Mr Willis Fleming of Chilworth Manor acted as his own huntsman. Two hinds were given chase.

SAND ROAD, WHITEPARISH. The original photograph (a postcard) was purchased at Frederick Hayes' shop in August 1912. The Wesleyan chapel, built in 1859, is to the right behind the large house. Josiah Lockyer is shoeing a horse in front of his blacksmith's shop.

WHITEPARISH CHILDREN near the old elm tree in 1912. The tree was sited at the corner of Parsonage meadow in Common Road. A few days after this picture was taken the tree was lopped and just the trunk remained.

THE OLD ELM TREE FIRE, Saturday, 21 September 1912. Miss Bristow was walking along Common Road when she saw smoke billowing out of the hollow trunk. The Romsey Fire Brigade arrived and extinguished the flames with water drawn from the White Hart pond.

THE KING'S HEAD AND THE FOUNTAIN INN, during the 1920s. William Bown was landlord of the Fountain Inn and Mrs Agnes Hamblin looked after the King's Head. A sign on her pub offers 'Good accommodation for cyclists'.

THE STREET AT WHITEPARISH in around 1912. Frederick Hayes' shop is to the right. He was an established baker, grocer, provisions merchant and stationer. Over the years he would have sold many picture postcards; this is one of them.

HAY CART AND RIDERS AT BRICKWORTH FARM, Whiteparish, during the First World War. Victor Parsons is on the cart with his children, Gerald, Dorothy and Mary.

PLOUGHING AT WHELPLEY FARM, Whiteparish, late 1940s. Gerald Parsons, Victor's son, is seen driving the rather unusual Crawley self-propelled plough. The tractor in the mid-distance is a Field-Marshall.

SELLING OFF THE OLD TRACTOR in the late 1940s. Victor Emanuel Parsons is seen negotiating the sale of his vintage Saunderson tractor at Ravenstone, Brickworth.

THRESHING WITH STEAM POWER AT WHELPLEY in around 1925. The threshing machine is being belt-driven by a steam traction engine. Victor Parsons is standing to the extreme right.

THE MARRIAGE OF BEN HOOPER AND DOROTHY PARSONS took place in 1929. The bride was the eldest daughter of Victor Emanuel Parsons who farmed at Brickworth (see also pages 52 and 54). Dorothy's youngest sister, Mary was the bridesmaid and Ben's younger brother, John, was the best man. The four are pictured here at Brickworth Farm.

A SCOUT MOTOR CAR ON PEPPERBOX HILL, after 1913. The 25.6 hp blue painted car, AM 2587, was owned by John White, the grocer of North Street, Wilton. The car was a special one; it was supplied with interchangeable bodies, seen here fitted with the rear platform version.

THE TRAVELLER'S REST TEA ROOM on Pepperbox Hill in the 1920s. A fine selection of drinks are displayed outside, including bottles of ginger pop and mineral water, a welcome sight for the motorists on this dusty summer road. Another picture of the café and more details over the page.

FLYING THE FLAG at the Traveller's Rest, during the 1920s. The establishment, operated by Thomas Pearman, was a very popular stopping place at the time, both for private and commercial traffic. Numerous enamel advertising signs were displayed on the tin hut, featuring Pratts, Redline and Shell motor spirits and Feathery Flake flour. A Chevrolette taxi from Bristol and three motor-cycle combinations from the Southampton area were parked outside when this picture was taken.

Milford, Petersfinger, Alderbury, Whaddon and Longford

MILFORD, FROM THE SPIRE OF SALISBURY CATHEDRAL in around 1885. This fascinating early photograph was taken by Sydney George Witcomb of Catherine Street. St Martin's Church, Milford goods station and the Railway Inn are all visible but many of the houses that are now in Tollgate Road (formerly Southampton Road) have yet to be built.

THE GODOLPHIN SCHOOL KINDERGARTEN, Milford Hill in 1913, known as Rose Villa. The headmistress at the time was Miss Douglas. A wagonette driven by a smartly dressed coachman can be seen pulling out of Milford Hollow.

EDITH WITCOMB AND PEGGY AT SHADY BOWER in the early 1890s. Edith, pictured in her dos-a-dos phaeton, was the daughter of Charles John Witcomb who opened a photographic studio in Milford Street, Salisbury in 1862. (Details of the family business appear on page 156.)

MILL HOUSE AT MILFORD in the late twenties, the home of the Ashford family. They moved here in 1921 after occupying Lower Farm at Britford for a number of years. Their Morris motor car can be seen in the drive.

MAJOR BERESFORD AT MILFORD in the 1930s. The major visited Milford many times between 1916 and 1935 when he accompanied about 120 boys from their home town of Southsea. The lads were members of the Beresford's private boys' brigade and every year they camped for 10 days in a barn behind Milford Mill. The little girl is Elizabeth Ashford who now lives with her mother at Mill House.

SOUTHERN COMMAND CLAIMS COMMISSION AT MILFORD MANOR, 1944. Colonel Mason is fourth from the right, in the front row, with Captain Burrage, seated third from the left and Captain Burrows, third from the right.

RICHARD GERRISH, from a photographic portrait of 1905. Sole proprietor, at the time, of Style and Gerrish silk merchants of Blue Boar Row, Salisbury. In 1873 he was invited to join the firm by his father, George, and 18 years later became a director. Richard lived at Milford Manor, known by the people of the village as Calico Castle because of the nature of his business.

SOUTHAMPTON ROAD, PETERSFINGER, 1913. Petersfinger Farm, to the right, has been worked by the Clarke family since 1922. In the distance, behind the trees is Hughenden, the home of Mrs Griffin whose husband, Frederick, was Mayor of Salisbury in 1887.

THE OLD COTTAGES AT PETERSFINGER in 1897. The four dwellings were destroyed by fire in the early 1920s when a spark from a passing train set light to the thatch. They were rebuilt some years later, but are virtually unrecognizable today.

HENRY BREWER AND FAMILY AT ALDERBURY, in around 1905. Mr Brewer served with the Wiltshire Constabulary for 26 years and for much of that time was a special duty constable at Longford Castle. Our picture shows the family in the garden of their Silver Street home.

NOT EXACTLY FOLLOWING IN FATHER'S FOOTSTEPS. Henry's son Walter served with the Salisbury City Police as a motor-cycle rider. His interest in cycles came early, in the photograph above he is sitting on a c. 1900 tricycle and in this photograph he looks very much at home astride a 1930 BSA police motor-cycle.

THE ALDERBURY VILLAGE BAND, at the new fountain which was installed in 1902. Left to right: Sam Hatcher, W. Earney, Alge Maidment, L. Fry, Jake Hatcher, A. Hatcher (Bandmaster), F. Thomas, H. Maidment, P. Hatcher, H.W. Maidment, H. Hatcher and G. Newson.

ALDERBURY MEN'S RED CROSS DETACHMENT, 1914–1918. The commander, to the right of the picture, is believed to be Alderbury schoolmaster, Arthur T. Freeman.

THE POST OFFICE IN OLD ROAD, Alderbury, in around 1956. Mr A.C. (Alge) Maidment who was sub-postmaster for over 30 years can be seen in the porch. The building is now a private dwelling known as Ye Old Post Office. The sturdy red telephone box itself will soon be a thing of the past for, thoughout the country, these are being phased out and replaced by modern variants designed to inhibit vandalism.

WILLIAM HICKMAN'S SHOP IN HIGH STREET, Alderbury, in around 1885. Soon after this photograph was taken parts of the original structure were demolished and new building work was carried out. This illustration and the one below, dated 1905, make an interesting comparison.

A FEW YEARS LATER AND LOOKING VERY DIFFERENT. A modern stone shop-front has been installed, with stables and a loft to the left and living accommodation to the right. By the mid-1950s it became a branch of the Salisbury Co-operative Society and was later converted to private houses.

ALDERBURY JUNCTION in around 1910. The line between here and the three mile post at Downton was always well maintained. The L & SWR held a competition each year and awarded prizes to the railwaymen with the best-kept length of track. Alderbury received awards in 1904 and 1905.

THE SIGNAL BOX AT ALDERBURY JUNCTION. The staff delighted in showing enthusiasts their signalling equipment. This young lad was being entertained in around 1907. At the time, the signalmen were M. Bowring, C. Fulford, B. Lawford, F. Newman and W. Russell.

THE BRITFORD AND ALDERBURY FERRY COTTAGE in 1897. The passenger landing stage is in the centre of the picture and the goods landing platform is off to the right. The ferry was operated by the Hazels and more recently by the Moulands who continued to take fares well into the 1960s.

JANE HAZEL CROSSING TO BRITFORD. When this snap was taken, just before the First World War, Jane had already celebrated her 72nd birthday. After the death of her husband in 1888 she managed the ferry entirely alone. The business had been in her husband's family since around 1800 and at the time of our picture it cost just 1*d*. to cross.

THE INAUGURATION OF THE ALDERBURY WATER SUPPLY, 17 November 1902, a coronation gift from the Earl of Radnor. Among those present were Lord and Lady Radnor, Viscount Folkestone and three little Ladies Bouverie. (Radnor copyright reserved.)

THE MILITARY AIRSHIP 'BETA' AT ALDERBURY, September 1910. A message on an original photograph states: 'I saw the "Beta" pass over our gardens several times. It went from Alderbury back to Aldershot in 60 minutes on Saturday', signed George Rogers.

THE STONE LAYING CEREMONY at the new Wesleyan School Room, Wednesday, 31 July 1912. One course of white bricks was laid by 60 local children. About 100 people then sat down to tea in a large marquee.

AN EVENING MEETING ON THE SAME DAY. Gypsy Smith, the well-known evangelist of the National Free Church Council, can be seen addressing a congregation of several hundred people.

REVD ROBERT SPARKE HUTCHINGS AND FRIENDS at Alderbury, in around 1893. Canon Hutchings, seated in the front row, was vicar of St Mary's, Alderbury, from 1865 to 1910. Do you recognize the location?

COURT HOUSE AT ALDERBURY in 1908, situated at the top of Tunnel Hill, opposite the Elementary School. The spire of St Mary's church can be seen in the distance, behind the coal waggon. One can only imagine the whereabouts of the coalman.

BREWERY DRAY AT THE FOUNTAIN, Alderbury, 1913. Drayman, George Gater, is pictured with Bobbie the cart-house. Both were employed by the Lamb Brewery Company of Frome, whose Salisbury office was at No. 12 Butcher Row. The manager and local agent was Henry Rowe.

SOUTHAMPTON ROAD, WHADDON in 1913. Mr Clarke can be seen to the left, in the garden at his home, The Capstone. The Primitive Methodist Chapel was completed in 1884.

WILLIAM OCCOMORE'S SHOP AT WHADDON, during the First World War. William Occomore was the local baker, grocer, provisions and general dealer. Little Ethel Occomore is standing on the right, near the entrance to the shop. The window advertisements feature Fry's chocolate and cocoa, also Lipton's and Lyon's tea. The enamel signs promote Rowland's Garage of Salisbury and Ephraim Hart's furniture bazaar of Southampton.

LONGFORD CASTLE, THE SEAT OF THE EARL OF RADNOR, as seen from the terrace in 1887. The castle, built in 1591 by Sir Thomas Gorges, resembles an older castle at Uranienborg in Sweden. The 4th Earl of Radnor was responsible for alterations, improvements and restoration in the 1870s.

THE HALL AT LONGFORD CASTLE in around 1890. To the left is the famous steel chair made at Augsburg by Thomas Rukers in 1577. The 2nd Earl of Radnor acquired it from Gustav Brander in the late 1700s.

LORD AND LADY RADNOR WITH THEIR CHILDREN in around 1910. From left to right: Katherine (Kitty); Peter, on Lady Julian Radnor's knee; Edward (Ned); Anthony; Helen, on Lord Radnor's knee; Bartholomew (Bartie); William (Willie) Viscount Folkestone, born 1895; Margaret; Jean (Jeanie) and Elizabeth (Betty). (Radnor copyright reserved.)

THE RIGHT HON. THE 6TH EARL OF RADNOR (Jacob Pleydell-Bouverie), from a photographic portrait of 1899. Born 8 July 1868. He sat in Parliament for the Wilton Division of Wiltshire as a Conservative from 1892 to 1900. He was elected Mayor of Folkestone for 1901 and 1902. He was married in 1891 to Julian, daughter of Charles Balfour. (Radnor copyright reserved.)

BARTIE IN HIS BABY CARRIAGE AT LONGFORD, from a photograph by Lady Julian Radnor, 1903. The wooden horses were linked to the front wheel and when the pushchair was in motion the horses galloped. (Radnor copyright reserved.)

JOHN ROBEY, HEAD GAMEKEEPER OF THE LONGFORD ESTATE, 1890. He stands with a double-barrelled shotgun under his arm and a dog at his side. His great-granddaughter is married to the present Lord Radnor's chaffeur. The photograph was taken by Sydney George Witcomb.

FISHING FROM THE WOODEN BRIDGE AT LONGFORD. From the time of this picture, c. 1895, up to 1911 records indicate that mostly grayling and trout were caught in the Chalke stream. The fish weighed in at one to five pounds.

LADY CYCLISTS AT LONGFORD in the 1890s. The five young men, lounging on the drive in front of the group, are out-numbered by more than seven to one, there are 36 ladies with 20 decorated bicycles. Decorated perambulators and cycles were regular features at the cottage garden shows.

FIRST AID DISPLAY BY ALDERBURY GIRL GUIDES, 1912. The 1st Alderbury Girl Guide Company was founded by Lady Katherine Pleydell-Bouverie in 1911. The girls are seen demonstrating their skills in the grounds of Longford Castle.

A SERVANTS' GATHERING AT LONGFORD CASTLE in 1893. Among the group are the house-, kitchen and lady's maids, the butler, gamekeepers, river keepers, gardeners, coachmen, stable boys, housekeepers, cooks, grooms, a carpenter, footmen, valets, a blacksmith, a plumber and a farrier.

THE GUESTS AT LORD AND LADY SKELMERSDALE'S WEDDING, 15 August 1889. The group is assembled at Longford for the wedding of Wilma Pleydell-Bouverie (the second daughter of the 5th Earl of Radnor) and Edward George Lord Skelmersdale, who later became 2nd Earl of Lathom.

THE LONGFORD CASTLE FIRE BRIGADE, early this century, pictured here with the hose and ladder carts. The brigade was founded by the Hon. Stuart Pleydell-Bouverie. In an emergency, the firemen (all full-time employees of the estate) were called to the station by the ringing of the tower bell. (Radnor copyright reserved.)

THE LONGFORD CASTLE MOTOR SHOOTING BRAKE, HR 4629. The 20 hp Ford Model T, registered during May 1921, was fitted with an estate car body, built by Harris and Son Coachworks in Winchester Street, Salisbury. The vehicle, used mainly as a general runabout, was frequently taken out for shooting parties.

LONGFORD COTTAGE GARDEN FESTIVAL AND SHOW, Wednesday, 16 July 1913. The estate firemen make ready their Merryweather steam fire engine, 'Vulcan'. Water was drawn from the river and jets directed at a burning replica of an eighteenth-century inn (pictured below).

THE FIRE IS SOON EXTINGUISHED. Fire-fighting comparisons were made, firstly with filthy leather buckets, then with the hand-drawn manual pump of 1800, followed by the horse-drawn manual of 1830, then the 1899 'Vulcan' steamer, and finally with the modern Commercar Simonis motor pump.

SECTION SIX

Charlton-all-Saints, Downton, Redlynch and Woodfalls

THE ROYAL MAIL VAN for the Downton and Redlynch area, 1913. The red and gold 28 hp Darracq van was leased from Sydney and Edgar Collett of the Catherine Street Garage, Salisbury. In September 1912 the *Salisbury Times* informed its readers that Messrs Collett had been awarded the contract to supply the very first motorized Royal Mail van to operate in the Salisbury postal district, a 14–16 hp Darracq. The larger model pictured here was put to work a few months later.

GEORGE HODGES' SHOP at Charlton-all-Saints, in the 1920s. You could buy a host of things at Hodges', it was the village post office, bakery, drapery, grocery and outfitters. The cattle in the photograph are being herded into the lane at the side of the vicarage.

CHARLTON-ALL-SAINTS VILLAGE in around 1913. The cottages on the left, Nos. 323–326, look quite similar today, although the dormer windows have gone. The school house can be seen on the far right.

THE BOROUGH AT DOWNTON, before 1905. A horse and cart can be seen outside the White Horse Hotel. The thatch on the white fronted house to the right was removed some years later and replaced with slates. To the left of this house is Boro Cross Cottage.

THE BOROUGH CROSS in 1900. The preaching cross, dating probably from the thirteenth century, has been restored several times during the last 200 years. The cost of repairs carried out in 1797 was met by the inhabitants of the borough. Renovation work 100 years later, however, was financed by Lady Radnor, to commemorate the Diamond Jubilee of Queen Victoria.

THE WHITE HORSE HOTEL AND READ'S BUTCHERY SHOP in 1908. At this time the two businesses were supervised by Mary Read, but by 1911 the hotel was managed by George Aylett. To the left, where the Co-op is now, Samuel Mitchell traded as a provisions merchant.

THE BOROUGH in 1884. At Charles Foster's warehouse, which can be seen in the distance, one could purchase bran, chaff, corn, flour, hay, meal and straw. On the right is Eliza Fanstone's rope and twine manufactory and on the left Charles Gregory's ironmongery.

THE HIGH STREET, after the Second World War. Chipperfield's grocery store and bakery is to the right, their Bedford delivery van advertises VITBE bread. The little vehicle parked outside the post office (nearest to the camera) is a Morris Minor GPO van (EXD 903).

THE DOWNTON WATER WAGON at Lodge Hill, in around 1910. Water carts were a common sight in many rural areas well into the 1940s. Water was taken from the rivers and then carried to the fields to fill the animal troughs.

THE POST OFFICE IN THE SQUARE during 1907 when Thomas Matthews was the sub-postmaster. A fine selection of picture postcards is displayed in the window, these could be delivered twice daily during the week, but once only on Sundays.

A FEW YEARS LATER. The post office had moved one door to the left by 1911, nearer to the Nobes and Hunt tannery. Two doors along to the right is Arthur Matthews' drapery store which is now a furniture shop and pharmacy.

MIZEN'S CYCLE DEPOT AT THE HEADLANDS, before 1908. John Wilfred Mizen assembled cycles using components supplied by firms such as Humber and Royal Enfield. By the 1920s, like many cycle dealers, he was an authorized motorcycle agent.

EASTMAN'S WICKER REPOSITORY in the High Street, in around 1907. Henry and George Eastman were well established by 1885 as manufacturers of wicker chairs, tables, flower stands and baskets. A post office occupies the site today.

MORGAN'S SHOP AT THE BOROUGH in 1919. The tobacconist's shop and newsagency was the backbone of Robert Morgan's business. His hairdressing salon, however, was not so active and only a small number of Downton's more elderly male residents can remember visiting Bob to have their hair cut. The motor car is a 1917, 16/20 hp, five-seater, grey and black painted Buick owned by Ms Emily Bonvalot of Wick House, Downton.

SHOPS IN THE BOROUGH four years earlier. Bob Morgan's 'Downton Toilet Saloon' is just right of centre with James Cleave's shop nearest to the camera. The old blacksmith's shop can be seen in the distance. The young lad pictured to the right was no fool, he kept his boots dry by wading through the flood waters on stilts.

THE FLOODS OF JANUARY 1915. Our picture shows Nos. 69 to 79 The Borough. Edith Stevens' grocery and ironmongery store, now the Halifax Building Society, is nearest the camera. For a day or two the streets were full of boats.

A FODEN SPEED-SIX STEAM LORRY, supplied to Chas. Mitchell and Sons in 1931. J.R. Dyer, who drove the truck for three years, had thoughtfully left a note on the back of our original photograph: 'A good wagon with maximum speed of over 50 mph'.

THE FIRST CAR IN DOWNTON, AM 768, with chauffeur James Churchill at the wheel. The 17/20 hp maroon tonneau was delivered to Dr William Whiteley of Hamilton House in February 1906. It was the third car to be sold by the Scout Motor Company of Salisbury (the first went to Dr William Ord).

AN ARTICULATED 10-TON LORRY, around the time of the Second World War. The tractor unit is a CI5 model from the ERF company of Sandbach, Cheshire. Its features include a coach-built cab and Gardner five-cylinder diesel engine. The semi-trailer was manufactured by Taskers of Anna Valley near Andover.

DOWNTON RAILWAY STATION, before the First World War. A south-bound train, pulled by an Adams class locomotive, can be seen in the distance. Trains of the L & SWR had been stopping here for nearly 100 years before Dr Beeching's axe fell in May 1964.

DOWNTON BAND MARCHING THROUGH THE SQUARE during King George's Silver Jubilee celebrations in May 1935. Henry Hayter was conductor at this time and his bandsmen included Frank Bundy, Les Forder, Burt Giles, and Reg Smith.

A CONCERT AT THE MOOT in around 1900. Mr Griffin was the violin-playing conductor and Una Palmer was the pianist. The musicians were: Walt Palmer, cello; Percy Eastman and Harry Palmer, violin; Fred Spreadbury, bass; William Poulden, cornet and also Messrs Alford, Anson and Phillpot.

DOWNTON AND DISTRICT FREE CHURCH DEMONSTRATION, Wednesday, 1 August 1906. Hundreds of schoolchildren and their teachers marched from the cricket field to Percy Taunton's fields at Redlynch. They are pictured here in the Borough, being led by the first of two bands.

DANCING AND A PASTORAL PLAY AT THE MOOT, Wednesday, 8 July 1908. The *Comedy of Errors* was performed by a company of Shakespearian players while 16 children from the Downton National School entertained with maypole dancing. It was all in aid of the church bells repair fund.

A DISASTROUS FIRE AT THE MOOT HOUSE, 1 November 1923. The alarm was raised at 5.30 a.m. when Mrs Carver saw smoke coming from the drawing room. Both Mrs Annie Wilson, the cook, and Gwendolyn Burham, the kitchen maid, suffered fatal injuries when they jumped 30 ft to the ground.

THE SALISBURY VOLUNTEER FIRE BRIGADE AT THE SCENE. The motor tender 'Fawcett' and a crew of six arrived just after 6 a.m. Immediately water was pumped from the river a quarter of a mile away. Despite commendable action by the firemen the house, owned by Newall Squarey, was destroyed within an hour.

A COTTAGE FIRE AT DOWNTON in around 1937. The cottage, which has since been demolished, was in the area of High Street and Lode Hill. The Salisbury Volunteer Fire Brigade promptly arrived to find the roof well alight. Firemen Albert Noyce, now retired, remembers falling to street level when the first floor collapsed, thankfully he was unhurt.

WICK HOUSE, DOWNTON, the residence of Henry Curtis Gallup. Horses and hounds were a common sight in the grounds for many years. On this particular day, before 1906, photographer James Jarvis has used them to good advantage, bringing life to his picture.

HENRY CURTIS GALLUP, the son of Henry Clay Gallup of London. Born in London on 24 October 1874, he was a keen rider and Master of the Wilton Hounds. Another photograph by James Jarvis of the Royal Central Photo. Company, Salisbury. These two pictures have been reproduced once before, in the book *Wilts and Dorset. Contemporary Biographies* which was published in 1906.

WILLIAM COOK WITH EMILY PLASKETT, his future bride. The photograph was taken in a field near Emily's home at Redlynch in around 1905. Photographer, Harry Marlow Rewse, of Salisbury was better known for his architectural photography.

GROVE LANE AT REDLYNCH in 1908. On the left are Prospect Place cottages, built in 1869 and still standing today. The Workman's Hall, Baptist Chapel, which can be seen in the distance is now a private dwelling. The cottages to the right have been replaced by modern houses.

QUAVEY ROAD AT REDLYNCH in 1910. Many of these houses have survived and very few changes have taken place here over the last 80 years. The white painted cottage in the distance, now called Blacksmiths, was formerly known as Old Policeman's Cottage.

THE NEW POST OFFICE AT REDLYNCH in 1914. Hugh Harrison was the sub-postmaster and his brother, Jabez, the blacksmith; the smithy can be seen on the extreme left. (Details of the Royal Mail van are printed on page 113.)

A TELEGRAPH BOY, name unknown. Two young lads were employed at the new post office, chiefly to deliver telegrams, but running errands and carrying out other odd jobs was all in a day's work. The boys were not a welcome sight during the First World War, for bad news usually arrived by telegram.

FREDERICK SCOVELL'S SHOP AND LOVER POST OFFICE at Besomer Drove in 1922. Clarence Scovell and his cousin, Beatrice, are pictured with the Ford Model T van. The building was sectioned off: the drapery department was to the left, footwear in the middle, grocery and post office on the right and the bakehouse at the back.

BRABROOK'S BUTCHERY AT MORGAN'S VALE in 1912. Ernest Brabrook offered an excellent delivery service. The local trips were made by boys on trade bikes and the more distant ones carried out by the Scout van (purchased second-hand in 1911 for £186 18s.10d.).

JOHN GREEN AND SONS' TIMBER YARD at Woodfalls in 1904. John Green is first on the left and his sons, Arthur, John junior and Wilfred are fourth, fifth and sixth respectively. The company ceased trading in 1975 after being active for more than 150 years. Greensmead estate now occupies this site.

THE OLD INN AT WOODFALLS in 1915, when Edwin Barnes was landlord. The duck pond in the foreground was drained several times in the early 1940s and finally levelled because people kept falling in during the blackout.

DELIVERING PRODUCE TO SALISBURY MARKET in March 1921. Harry Crouch, the market gardener of Whiteshoot, Redlynch, sold his crops on a stall in the Market Place. His Berliet canvas-topped truck can be seen parked in the Canal.

THE REDLYNCH, DOWNTON AND SALISBURY MOTOR CARRIER of the early 1920s. Frank Newman operated the service on Tuesdays and Saturdays using this Daimler which is pictured outside the Salvation Army soldiers' hostel. The van (formerly a private car) is fitted with an unsuitable body rescued from a larger vehicle.

THE CRAFT OF BESOM MAKING at Hillcrest, Loosehanger, around the time of the First World War. Frank Bryant is standing behind John Newman who can be seen working with a rip hook. John's brothers Charles and Walter are to the right.

WALTER NEWMAN WITH HIS HORSE AND CART in around 1914. Many of the besoms made by Joseph Newman and Sons were delivered to towns all over the south and west. On this occasion a photographer spotted Walter when he was in the Copner Bridge area of Portsmouth.

TRAFALGAR HOUSE, the seat of the Right Hon. Earl Nelson, built on the present site at Standlynch in 1733. Formerly Stanlynch House and Park and, before 1814, the property of H. Dawkins. The large brick built mansion stands in a park and pleasure grounds covering an area of 80 acres, it featured a private chapel.

Britford, Bodenham, Nunton, Odstock, Homington and Coombe Bissett

STARTING THE LAST LAP with photographer, Frank Witcomb. Our photograph of 1935 shows Frank Sydney Witcomb of Catherine Street with his new Austin Light 12/4 on New Bridge at East Harnham (the bridge was completed and opened just a few months earlier). W. Goddard and Co. supplied the car.

JAMES OATES AND FAMILY OF BRITFORD, from a portrait of 1847. This paper photograph is the earliest example of its type known to the author. James, who was churchwarden at Britford for a number of years, has his five year old son William on his knee. William was 93 years of age when he died in 1935.

BRITFORD HIGH ROAD in 1916, the main road from Salisbury to Downton. A pair of cottages to the left were knocked down a few years ago and several bushes and a tree on the right have now gone to make way for a lay-by.

BRIDGE FARM AT BRITFORD in 1897. Herbert Richard Harding was working the farm at the time of our picture, he succeeded John Gay Attwater who had been farming here since the 1880s. The area has changed very little, although the three-arched bridge has been replaced by a modern one of single span design.

BRITFORD CELEBRATING THE CORONATION OF KING GEORGE V on Friday, 23 June 1911. Everyone gathered outside the school at 11 a.m. before marching behind the Odstock band to attend a service at St Peters. In the afternoon a carnival was held in Poulton's Meadow. Margaret Ashford can be seen, just right of centre, dressed as a fairy.

BODENHAM POST OFFICE AND GROCERY STORE during the 1920s when Loftus Morell was the sub-postmaster. Incoming mail from Salisbury was received around 4 a.m. and deliveries commenced at 6.45 a.m. and 2 p.m. An early example of a cigarette machine can be seen to the right of the door.

BODENHAM VILLAGE DURING THE FIRST WORLD WAR. At the time of writing the future of the Baptist Chapel on the left is uncertain. Local people fear that it may soon be converted into a private residence. Three cottages opposite were remodelled some years ago to create a single dwelling, now known as Three Thatches.

NEW HALL AT BODENHAM before the fire of 1881. Alfred Buckley's house (now a private hospital) was devastated by fire on Saturday, 25 June. The Longford Castle, and Salisbury Municipal Fire Brigades could do little to save the building. Hundreds of bottles of vintage wine were destroyed.

NUNTON COTTAGE in 1920, occupied by R.E. Macan until around 1925 when Mrs E. Cole moved in. Mrs Cole was a Justice of the Peace and owned one of only four or five motor cars in the village at this time.

NUNTON VILLAGE, from a picture postcard dated 1907. Riverside Cottages are on the right, in front of George Haskell's brewery, shop and stables. The stables, occupied later by James Henry Chown, were pulled down some years ago.

GEORGE HASKELL'S NUNTON BREWERY in 1906. 'Licenced Brewer and Retailer of Beer. Dealer in Foreign Cigars and Tobaccos.' Now known as the Radnor Arms. The little cottage to the right was demolished in the 1960s, its last occupant was Frank Feltham, the Odstock blacksmith.

ODSTOCK CROSSROADS in 1911. The Yew Tree Inn, managed by Alfred Lock, can be found up the hill, to the right, near Frank Feltham's blacksmith's shop. The cottages on the left still exist but have since been extended and improved.

COTTAGES AT ODSTOCK in 1910. The little girls are playing near one of the village water pumps, outside the dwellings now known as Orchard Cottage and Leeward Cottage. The houses in the distance have gone but the water pump survives.

'DAD, UNCLE JIM, SALLY AND REX' in around 1912. The information is recorded on the back of the original photograph, but unfortunately the writer failed to mention the surnames of Dad and Uncle Jim. Do you recognize them? The message continues: 'What do you think of the cart, Jim made it himself. Dad took it to Salisbury on Tuesday and then came back to Homington in the same day. Mrs Rothery has sent some more of her honey', signed, Mary. (The cart was probably converted from a Victorian tricycle or perhaps the wheels had been salvaged from penny-farthing bicycles.)

MOTOR DELIVERY OF PROVISIONS to Dogdean and Homington in 1909. The van, built by the Star Cycle & Motor Company of Wolverhampton, was owned by P. Hart & Son of Butcher Row, Salisbury. Deliveries were made all over the district out as far as Salisbury Plain.

'THE SHEPHERDS PRIDE' AT DOGDEAN in 1909. The ewes were the stock-in-trade of Arthur Tyrwhitt-Drake of Dogdean farm, a well-known farmer and breeder of pedigree Hampshire Down sheep.

HOMINGTON VILLAGE during the First World War. The church of St Mary the Virgin is to the left opposite Box Tree Cottage. At one time the village shop was to be found in one of the cottages on the right.

SALISBURY ROAD AT COOMBE BISSETT, between the wars. PC Beard is cycling past William Arnold's Fox and Goose Inn. The site between Bridge House and the pub was cleared a few years ago to make way for a car park.

QUEEN VICTORIA'S JUBILEE CELEBRATIONS AT COOMBE BISSETT, in 1887 or 1897. The whole village turned out to enjoy the entertainments. The men sat down to dinner in the morning and the women and children had afternoon tea. The photograph, taken near the church, shows everyone wearing their Sunday best.

PEACE CELEBRATIONS AT COOMBE BISSETT, Saturday, 2 August 1911. The children of Coombe, Homington and Stratford marched from the school to the sports field (owned by W. Parsons). The event formerly planned for 19 July was postponed due to inclement weather.

THE HORRIFIC FIRE NEAR CHURCH FARM, Wednesday, 2 July 1924. The blaze started in a garage at Ernest Thorne's farm and spread rapidly to nearby buildings. The Salisbury Volunteer Fire Brigade dispatched 14 firemen on two motor pumps; 'Fawcett' and 'Frank Baker'.

SCENES OF DEVASTATION the following day. Eight buildings were destroyed including five cottages, a barn, a shed and a garage (even the car it contained could not be saved). Thousands of pounds' worth of damage was done and 17 people were made homeless.

CHILDREN'S SPECIAL SERVICE MISSION AT COOMBE BISSETT, between the wars. This was a common sight in many rural parts well into the 1930s. Herbert Lawes can be seen sitting behind the clock, he was the Coombe Bissett carrier for a number of years.

COOMBE BISSETT BELLRINGERS on Whit Monday, 12 June 1905. Standing left to right are: J. Farris, Reginald Mundy, S. Lawes, G. Farris, E. Bryant and Charlie Mundy. Seated are Revd C. Wood and J.C. Chalke.

THE BAPTIST CHAPEL AT COOMBE BISSETT CROSSROADS, late last century. The stone laying ceremony took place on Wednesday, 31 October 1894. The first stone was formally laid by Vicountess Folkestone on behalf of her husband who was unwell. The stone was never altered and still displays the Viscount's title. A second stone was then laid by the Revd George Short BA, president of the Baptist Union. The building, designed by A.C. Bothams, was completed within a few weeks by Messrs Cabel and Mark Phillips of Waterloo Gardens, Salisbury. The site was provided free of charge by the Earl of Radnor, but material and labour costs of £350 had to be found.

CLASS TWO AT COOMBE BISSETT NATIONAL SCHOOL in 1903. The children are pictured with assistant teachers Diana Drake and Grace Jenkins. Charlie Farris is seated second from the right in the front row and his chums, Albert Morris and Tom Wright, are standing on the same side at the end of the second and third rows.

JOSEPH DRAKE 1864–1940. Joe was a popular character who lived a very active life. He was Headmaster of the National School from 1888–1923 (his daughter Diana can be seen to the left in the picture above). For many years he was choirmaster and organist at St Michael and All Angels Church.

THE COOMBE BISSETT BRASS BAND, early this century. Sadly the original photograph is not annotated and the players' names are not known to us.

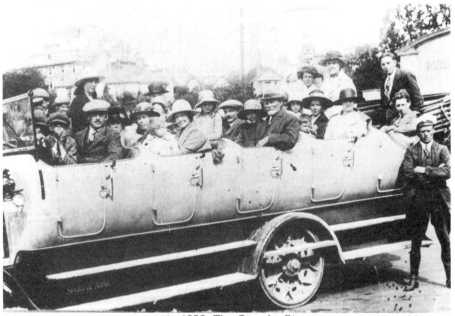

A CHARABANC TRIP TO THE SEASIDE in 1923. The Coombe Bissett party are pictured here at Bournemouth. Everyone is wearing a hat: you may wonder how they kept them on when riding with the hood down? The answer is in the picture: 'SPEED 12 MPH'.

QUEEN MARY VISITING HARVARD HOSPITAL in around 1942. The hospital was set up by the Americans in 1939 to last for the duration of the war. The prefabricated complex had a new lease of life, however, when it later became the Common Cold Unit of the Medical Research Council. The last volunteers will arrive in the summer of this year, 1989.

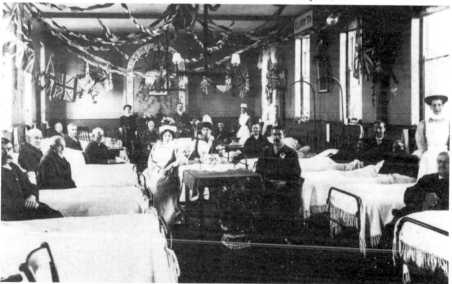

CHRISTMAS AT THE COOMBE ROAD WORKHOUSE in 1912. Mr and Mrs William Clark had recently replaced Richard and Emma Lyle as master and matron. The chaplain was the Revd Thomas John Woodall of Britford and Dr L.S. Luckham was medical officer. Nurse Lilian Lewis can be seen on the extreme right.

SALISBURY CATHEDRAL, FROM BOURNEMOUTH ROAD. (15)

THE LAST LEG OF OUR JOURNEY, and we return to Salisbury via New Bridge Road. The changes here are not as significant as some we have encountered on our journey through the villages and hamlets in this South East corner of Wiltshire. This view dates from 1934 and we notice that Jack Miles' Harnham Garage is on the left, but the houses beyond are something of the future.

SECTION EIGHT

Photographers

WITCOMB'S STUDIO at No. 10 Catherine Street, Salisbury in 1903. Two studios were set up in the building; from 9 a.m. until dusk a 'Daylight Studio' was in use and then each evening until 8 p.m., the 'Electric Light Studio' was available for portraiture.

FRANK SYDNEY WITCOMB, pictured above and right, was the grandson of Charles John Witcomb who started a photographic studio in Milford Street, Salisbury in 1862. After five years the firm moved to a new studio in Catherine Street when Sydney, Frank's father, joined the business. Frank's photographic career lasted through the 1920s and up to the time of the Second World War. The illustration top right is reproduced from the back of a carte-de-visite photograph.

CHARLES HENRY MAY AT HOME in around 1907. Charlie, as he was known, lived at William Selway's dairy farm at Gomeldon Hill. From there he travelled all over Wiltshire, Hampshire and Dorset taking photographs of village life. Kathleen, his daughter, started taking photographs when she was 16 and continued to do so until the 1950s. Charlie and his family moved later to Swanwick, Hampshire. Many of the illustrations used in this book are his.

If you like this Pictorial Post Card call and see our Large and Varied Assortment.

All 1d. Cards 7 for 6d.

Actresses, 2d., 3d. and 4d. each.

H. C. MESSER, Photographer,

Also STAND 25,
Wilts Agricultural Show.
     29, Castle Street, Salisbury.

HORACE CHARLES MESSER, 1866–1936. Horace was a very active character and his print output between 1897 and 1920 was probably the greatest in the area. His forte was social photography and for many years his photographs were reproduced in newspapers and other publications. He was general secretary of the Salisbury YMCA from 1897 until 1908 and Salisbury police photographer from 1897 to 1916. These days his prints and postcards are much sought after by collectors.

F. FUTCHER AND SON'S SHOP at No. 19 Fisherton Street, Salisbury. This family business began from a studio at No. 36 High Street, Warminster in 1883. The Salisbury branch which followed was an immediate success and is now in its 85th year of trading. Gerald Tony Futcher, the founder's grandson, is the present proprietor.

FATHER AND SON, FREDERICK AND HAROLD FUTCHER. Frederick was a gifted photographer who turned out work of a very high standard. His skills were handed down to his son, Harold, who started taking photographs in the early 1920s.

ACKNOWLEDGEMENTS

In particular I must thank Mr Peter Saunders for giving me the idea in the first place and for allowing me to compile this album which he had planned to put together himself. As Curator of Salisbury Museum I also wish to thank him for giving me access to the museum photographic collection and library. Equally I am grateful to Ann and Geoffrey Crowe for the fine introduction and for supplying me with ideas for the captions when inspiration was lacking.

The following individuals and organizations have helped in many different ways. Some by sharing knowledge, others by lending photographs. Sincere thanks to each and every one.

Castle Cameras for donating the photographic paper from which the copy-prints were made. Historians and private collectors: Alan Alexander, Miss Pat Blake, Keith Chapman, Patrick Coggan, Wesley Cole, Bill Garrett, Frederick James, John Judd, E. Arthur Maidment, Austin Parsons, Bernard Pavey, Major John Shave, David Smith, Jim Smith, Dave Underwood, Chris Walker and David Ward. Longford Castle: The Right Hon. The Earl of Radnor for giving access to private family albums and to Archivist Mrs Nancy Steele for supplying historical information. *Salisbury Journal and Times* series; Gareth Weekes, Editor, and Daff Marriage, Chief Sub-editor, for giving me access to old copies of their newspapers and for generous publicity. Salisbury Reference Library: Edward Boyle, Miss Gillian Roberts and Mrs Carol Hausner who never fail to give help when it is needed. *Southern Evening Echo*; Nigel Parkes, chief Salisbury reporter, for publicity. The *Avon Advertiser*; Ian Johnson, Editor, for publicity. Wiltshire Record Office; Ken Rogers for allowing me to reproduce photographs, and to the staff who are always so helpful.

Alderbury Womens Institute • Mrs Margaret Ashford • Mrs Maurine Atkinson • Mrs Gwen Bolt • Eddie Boswell • Bourne Valley Historical and Record Society • Miss Mary Bridle • Roger Brown • Frank Burwell • Cyril Churchill William Clarke • Cedric Curtis • Mrs Joyce Dibben • Gerald Futcher Miss Ruth Gay • Mrs Vivienne Grant • Mrs L. Green • Philip Green Mrs Elizabeth Hale • Mrs Beatrice Harris • Miss E.M. Harris • Mrs M. Harris Mrs B. Harrison • Charles Jago • Miss Gwen Joyce • Ron Kerley Mrs Violet Lock • Mrs O. Maidment • Mrs C.V. Marshall • Mrs Mary Moody Mrs Josephine Musslewhite • Roy Newman • Roy Newton • Albert Noyce Mrs Kathleen Parsons • Simon Parsons • Mrs Kathleen Pearson Mrs Dora Pike • Miss Clarrie Price • Miss M. Quinton • H.B. Radcliffe Mrs Margaret Rose • Mrs Margaret Sanger • Mrs V. Smith • Keith Thompson Mrs Mary Topp • Mrs Amy Turner • Cyril Weeks • Mrs Daisy West Mrs Kathleen Meopham-Wilson • John White • Ivor Whitlock • Leslie Whitmarsh and Stanley Witcomb.